DISPUTE RESOLUTION VIA NEGOTIATION

A Useful Guide to Resolve Disputes Quickly & Effectively!

BY ANKIT VERMA

ISBN 979-8-88805-997-5

Dispute Resolution Via Negotiation

Insights into dispute resolution through negotiation, my experiences and what it taught me.

Dedication

I would like to dedicate this book in the memory of the most influential person who shaped the way I think and look at the world. A very simple man with a strong character and clear view of the world. He inspired me to follow my dreams, find solutions and opportunities in adversity and to add value to the world. My late father Mr. Rabindra Nath Verma

Contents

Acknowledgments

A word of thanks to all those whose work, research, and support help me write this book.

I am extremely grateful to my family that has helped me shape myself into being able to write this book. It would be a crime to miss out on all my teachers throughout my educational and professional life. I thank them for helping me find my space and discover my abilities and for all the guidance they gave me over the years to help bring the best out of me.

I cannot miss acknowledging the team of Private Court that has influenced me with their dedication and all the assistance that they have provided in gathering information and tabulating the same into a structure that I present here today. Special mention to Mahadev Gitte, Vishal Tiwari & Prarthana Warrier for their invaluable contribution in putting this book together.

Lastly, a special thanks to all parties, interacting with whom I learned this fine art

Chapter 1

Evolution & Acceptance of ADR

The rise in trade and commerce on a global scale signalled an evident spike in commercial disputes. The need across the international borders was to adopt a system that would facilitate international dispute settlement speedily and avoid delays typical of the international legal doctrine. Article 36 clause 2 of the International Court of Justice statute highlights the limited control of International Courts over executing, enforcing, and overarching international legal order. The unclear structure of international law favoured the need for a more suitable and flexible system to settle a dispute than to impose a defined dogma, barely recognised by the states as a go-to reckoner of their international behaviour.

In 1985, the United Nations Commission on International Trade Law (UNCITRAL) adopted the UNCITRAL Model Law of International Commercial Arbitration on International Commercial Arbitration (with amendments as adopted in 2006). This model, designed to assist States in reforming and modernising their laws on the arbitral procedure to take into account the particular features and needs of international commercial arbitration, was a massive step forward in resolving commercial disputes among many international cooperative houses.

An important feature of the model is that it made the concept of Arbitration and Conciliation more admissible to be recognized for universal application. America, Canada, the UK, Hong Kong, Australia, New Zealand, and European countries along with more and more countries, followed suit and imbibed this in their legislative system, respectively.

Today, ADR is one of the most resourceful tools for dispute management and is recognised as an official and statutory recourse for the resolution of ongoing litigation.

With the growing acceptance of ADR globally in the world of commercial disputes, coupled with the challenges faced internally with a constant rise in unresolved litigation cases, it was time for the Indian Government to open its eyes and adapt to this evolving new form of resolving disputes.

The Arbitration and Conciliation Act 1996, is India's official answer to the burgeoning need of ADR as an official and statutory recourse for the resolution of ongoing litigation. The passing of this Act is an honest attempt to make arbitration a preferred mode of settlement of commercial disputes and make India a hub of international commercial arbitration. Committed to the mission, the Government constantly evolved the Act to cater to the ever-Changing nature and seamless functioning, resulting in two amendments in 2015 and 2019.

This Act regulates domestic and International arbitration in India, and the settlement constitutes a final and binding agreement that is enforceable in a court of law. The Government is constantly putting efforts to ensure that the international ADR framework functions smoothly alongside the Indian legal regime. In other words, the government has made an impactful move to promote ADR methods wherein pre-institutional mediation has been made compulsory for commercial disputes apart from the conventional Sec 89.

While India has made significant progress in improving the functionality, dependability, and efficacy of ADR mechanisms in recent years, ADR is not a new concept when it comes to resolving disputes here.

Our Deep Cultural Advantage Roots

As one of the oldest civilizations, we had developed systems to resolve disputes, which were quite complex. If one studies the ancient socio-economic structures of society as early as 2500 BCE, the Indus Valley civilization had its own systems of dispute resolution through the unified approach of Kulas and Serins, which are comparable to the trade unions of today. The Indian society mostly remained unchanged through the times with the development of newer religions like

Buddhism and Jainism preaching non-violence and avoiding conflicts. The resolution of disputes at the first levels was achieved on this basis more often than not.

The more recent development of the Panchayat system of local governance during the period of kingdom-based rules also helped the resolution of disputes at the first levels. The composition of these panchayats was one of the biggest contributing factors. The panch (The Five) were representatives of all the four varnas in the village with a fifth member from the Adivasis of the surrounding woods. This ensured that all parties of the region were represented, and in case of disagreements, a platform was made available for every faction to be heard. This system has continued to exist and has become a part of the modern governing systems.

It was after the advent of British Rule that the justice delivery system in India was institutionalised with the establishment of courts and tribunals. It was the slag in delivering justice and the urgency of resolution that saw the emergence of various modes of dispute resolution mechanisms under the ADR domain.

Since then the governments of the past and present have encouraged ADR, and the code of civil procedure encourages parties to a dispute to adopt mediation as a route to settle disputes, even if it is headed to a heated litigation. Court-sponsored mediation has been offered in most cases of civil dispute, and the incorporation of compulsory counselling sessions in divorce cases is an example of how mediation is considered necessary even in cases of family disputes.

The Application of ADR

It has been observed that most disputes occur due to misunderstandings, cultural differences, differences in the methods of trade, or mere lack of communication. While litigation draws these differences to expand as all parties concerned are only trying to prove their standpoint, meditation and ADR generally help more effective communication between parties and make them more receptive to understanding other viewpoints. In certain cases, disputes occur due to malafide intent even in such cases, mediation often brings out the real reasons for such disputes and often exposes parties who have dealt in bad faith.

In due course of time, ADR became a preferred choice and found its recognition in resolving family disputes, matrimonial disputes, disputes arising between people residing in the same society, disputes with the neighbour arising due to parking, nuisance, noise complaint, etc. In fact, these disputes made up a large chunk of pending litigation in court, and ADR was found to be a better alternative for resolution.

Most courts subscribe to mediation prior to litigation in cases as varied as property disputes to disputes over patents and IP. What is seen is that such negotiations have a success ratio of close to 50% which leads to a less burdened legal system and saving of massive amounts in fees for the parties involved.

Recently, there has been a spike in the acceptance of ADR as a system of dispute resolution in the corporate world. Though arbitration was always mentioned as a clause in every agreement, it was seldom looked upon as a means to negotiate a consensus, but the pandemic seems to have brought about a big change in the attitude of companies and individuals alike. Most agreements saw a breach, and deliveries on many agreed terms were either altered or remained unfulfilled, bringing disputes among parties to a record high, but what was also observed was that most parties to these disputes were open to dialogue, and they choose mediation over litigation. In the post-pandemic era, what has now dawned on us is that this change seems here to stay. Legal departments of companies and even banks and NBFCs have now turned to mediation as a way of resolving issues.

Mediation brings about a human angle to the agreement or the disputed part of the agreement. Mediation now allows both the aggrieved and the defendant to have their sides heard. Arbitrators and mediators of the new world are now conscious of the challenges of both sides and are now awarding judgements that are more and more acceptable to both parties to the contract.

The acceptance of ADR has also been brought about by the changes in the attitude of the judiciary, with courts now looking at training their own staff to handle mediations and arbitrations more effectively. In a groundbreaking move, the government, in 2015, made amendments to Section 12A, where a pre-litigation arbitration is mandated. This is an acknowledgement of the fact that as a society we are now looking at resolving civil disputes through mediation and are ready to avoid long-drawn battles.

The effective use of online tools have also helped in the way mediations are handled and also is allowing parties over distant geographies come together easier even in cases where arbitration boundaries are pre determined and adhered to. This has also improved the number of cases that are being managed through the day by a mediator and resolutions are arrived at even quicker.

Thin Line

ADR has proved to be the most appropriate method to resolve disputes in most of the cases and is gaining massive acceptance on a global-scale by the day, yet there are some limitations that need to be considered before adopting this method.

- In cases where a judgement passed by the court is needed, it will play the role of a precedent for future reference. This is especially appropriate in cases where public interest is involved.

- When parties enter into ADR through negotiation or Mediation, or when an award is arrived at through arbitration, in the bargain, they end up giving their right to litigation except in certain exceptional cases as the final decision through the ADR channels is binding.

- In some cases, the agreements arrived at through ADR are complex and may not be as admissible compared to an order passed by the court or tribunal order. However, such agreements can be rendered binding by seeking further legal advice or if the agreement is given consent by the court or tribunal.

- Though the success rate of ADR is on an upswing, at times, the entire ADR process and the effort behind it fail i.e. the parties fail to arrive at a mutually decided settlement or agreement. In this case, litigation is the next step that is followed. The time, effort and cost expended on ADR seem completely futile and an added expense.

- Since ADR is a much speedier process compared to legal action, there are times when the parties in dispute do not disclose all the facts leading to a settlement or an award that may be improper.

Social attitudes and attitudes of businesses are now more conducive to adopting ADRas means of dispute resolution. The legislative changes and the attitudes of courts are also paving in the same direction. Lawyers, law firms, legal advisors, etc. are directing efforts to train themselves and their teams to develop skills in mediation. The post-pandemic phase has brought about changes in the way we function as a whole, and this acceptance has also impacted negotiations and mediations as now geographical distances and time are not much of a concern.

Chapter 2

3 Facets of ADR: Negotiation, Mediation and Arbitration

It has been established that negotiations are the best means to resolve any dispute, and making this a part of the formal business environment probably is the way forward. There are established principles to manage a dispute without moving into litigation, and it would be beneficial for us to look at the options that parties to a dispute can take. In this chapter, we endeavour to take a quick look at some of them

Negotiations generally are an informal arrangement often undertaken between the disputed parties. It may be initiated at any time by either side. The outcome of these sorts of negotiations is not binding and is more often than not executed on a good faith basis. In cases of negotiations, the time and place of the negotiations are not dependent on any law but on the convenience of the parties involved.

The parties may involve a third party to help in the negotiations; generally, such an agent is known to both sides and is considered an acceptable conduit. Examples of negotiations used for dispute resolution can be found in our day-to-day life, where family disputes are settled by means of negotiations. Negotiations are generally undertaken only when all parties involved volunteer to come forth for a dialogue. These discussions are usually not confidential and are at best private to a group of individuals.

Negotiations also may be undertaken at an international level. These generally are not disputes that arise after an action but before a certain action is preempted to be detrimental to another country. For example, the building of Dams in one country may be disagreeable with another country, and negotiation can be set forth to clarify each other's stands. Negotiations are also agreed upon during wars between countries that are in the war and a third-party country. The recent negotiation between India and Ukraine to evacuate Indians during the war is a great example of this.

Negotiations and their success depend on a few factors:

1. *Acceptance*: All parties in the negotiation should feel the need to come together and resolve the issue at hand. This creates an atmosphere of acceptance of each other's views and also allows disputing sides to understand what are the needs or apprehensions of the other's side.

2. *Flexibility*: All the parties involved in the negotiation should be flexible and accommodative to the other sides. This may be as simple as

time constraints or the preconditions to such discussions.

3. ***Structured approach***: A structured approach to a discussion will ensure that all aspects of a dispute are discussed, and no omission would make any side to a disagreement feel that they have been dealt a bad hand.

Mediation, as the word suggests, happens to be when an external party is assigned the task of bringing a consensus between the disagreeing factions to a dispute. A mediator is generally a person who is considered acceptable to all parties involved in a dispute; this person may be an acquaintance, a friend in case of family disputes or as such disagreement- handling-professionals like lawyers or chartered accountants in case of commercial disputes, or an organisation like the UNO in cases of disputes between countries. The mediator needs to be essentially unbiased and competent to understand all factors of a dispute. Mediation can be voluntary or legally mandated. Generally, mediations are more formal affairs with a stipulated time and location for a discussion. Mediation outcomes are binding to the parties once an agreement is reached, more so in cases of court-mandated mediations.

It is necessary for the mediator to be aware of the conditions under which the parties are drawn to the table for a discussion. Assessing the relationship of the parties to a dispute and the impact on each from the outcome of such mediation needs to be sensitively analysed to ensure success. For example, parties to negotiation might have a relationship that is a one-time affair, which means that they have had no earlier engagements and will not have any further relations. In such cases, the parties may not be open to giving out too many concessions, and the mediation will have to be based on facts and ground realities. In cases where there is an ongoing transactional relationship between parties, more often than not, affinity and the longevity of relations will warrant a concessional approach on all sides.

The mediator needs to also be aware of the goals of the parties to a dispute and what they would accept as a settlement. For example, a bank that has lent money would want to ensure a minimum return on their receivables, whereas the borrower would like to see a waiver of penalties. The mediator also needs to be aware of all contractual obligations and responsibilities and the concurrent laws of the land to ensure a successful and binding outcome of a negotiation.

The intent of the parties to a contract or a dispute plays a major role in the outcome of mediation. It would not be prudent on the part of a mediator to assume that all parties to a discussion are in it with good faith and have also conducted themselves with honesty in all transactions. Generally, parties who have entered a dispute with malicious intent would try to derail negotiations till they have achieved their goals. The mediator, through careful inspection, should try to be aware of such parties in any negotiation.

The Steps involved in mediation are as under:

- *Preparation*: The mediator needs to be prepared and have a clear understanding of all the factors involved in a dispute. He needs to be aware of the legal precedence wherever applicable and also, as mentioned earlier, the relationship between parties to a dispute and their possible outlook toward an outcome

- *Laying of Ground Rules*: The mediator needs to lay down ground rules for the mediation to ensure equal and unbiased opportunity is given to all sides of the dispute. Besides, this would also ensure that the proceedings remain as cordial as possible and are drawn more towards a settlement and not an argument.

- *Find Clarification and Justification*: The mediator needs to allow clarifications and justifications to all sides by providing ample chance for rebuttals and also make a note of these to deduce the mentality of the parties. This process is also useful in determining the goals of the parties involved in the process.

- *Bargaining and Solution Providing*: It happens, at times, once the intent of both parties has been established by the mediator, the mediator may have to propose concessions on any side to reach a conclusion. Generally, if the resolution is based on natural law and human considerations, solutions offered become more acceptable to all sides of a dispute

- **_Closure_**: While mediation discussions can be long drawn and pendulumic in nature, it is for the mediator to direct it to closure and make parties arrive at a consensus. In cases of court-mandated meditations or formal mediation, it is also the responsibility of the mediator to document the agreed terms to a mediation outcome and ensure adherence to the same.

Arbitration is different from mediation for the fact that in the case of arbitration, unlike meditation, there is a side in whose favour a decision is made, so there might be a winning side and a losing side. Arbitration is generally undertaken where there is a contract entered into or there is a legal jurisprudence to a dispute.

An arbitrator, in most cases, is appointed or directed by courts or any similar authorities. An arbitrator need not essentially be a lawyer but can also be an expert in the relevant field. For example, a dispute over a technology agreement may be arbitrated by an IT expert.

Arbitrations are a formal affair, and the outcomes are binding on all sides involved; however, these are open to litigation in case any of the parties feel aggrieved by the awarded outcome. Generally, all agreements carry the clause of jurisdiction for the arbitration clause. Arbitration might also be called in cases where there is no pertinent agreement but where there is a deemed one nonetheless. Examples of such arbitration are seen in international courts. Arbitration usually involves two parties: the claimant and the respondent.

It is the claimant who initiates the arbitration.

The Steps involved in PrivateCourt Arbitration are as follows:

- *Claim Form Submission:* PrivateCourt has designed a "Pre-defined Format" to write claims to be shared with the Respondent. All the relevant details, including a summary of the reason for the dispute, are attached to this Pre-defined Claim Form.

- *Arbitrator Selection:* The Claimant and Respondent both have the opportunity to choose a Solo Arbitrator from the Panel of PrivateCourt.

- *Cost:* As both parties have already paid for Dispute Resolution Paper, they don't have to bear the cost of Judgement/Arbitration Process/Award.

- *Claim Submission:* The Preformatted Claim form is designed to cover all the dispute points that make it a complete Claim form; hence, without the need for any lawyer or legal expertise, the claimant can fill the form and generate a Claim.

- ***Negotiation Phase:*** In the following 15 days after Claim submission, PrivateCourt's Negotiation team follows up with both parties to collect all the necessary legal documents that will be required for Negotiation and to understand their individual response to the claim.

In the meantime, the process of Negotiation is initiated, where the parties are required to sit across the table or attend the online hearing scheduled and attempt to settle the matter at this stage itself.

Conciliation Phase: In case Negotiation results are futile, then the Negotiation team submits a Summary Report with the Claim Form to the Conciliator which will lead to the next process of Conciliation that is covered in the next 30 days.

During the Conciliation process, the Conciliator (subject matter expert), after studying reports in detail, attempts to make both parties come to a common point of understanding and try to settle the dispute midway.

Arbitration Phase: In case Conciliation fails, a Conciliation Summary Report is drafted by the Conciliator, which is submitted along with the

Negotiation summary report and Claim Form to the Arbitrator, initiating the Arbitration process.

Once the dispute reaches the Arbitration stage, the Arbitrator studies the matter in detail. In case the Arbitrator needs the Parties to answer a few questions or needs further information, he can request so via email or during the hearing session. Upon receiving the information, the Arbitrator decides on the matter within the next 60 days.

Judgement: The Judgement arrived at by the Arbitrator is first presented to a Panel of Subject Matter Experts for approval to ensure a correct decision is made, and Justice is delivered.

PrivateCourt ensures the entire Arbitration process is conducted strictly in a neutral environment as many parties are involved, and the Arbitrator cannot be motivated by any team to take any decision.

Riders of Alternate Dispute Resolution

- The undenied perk of opting for Alternate Dispute Resolution is that the entire process is essentially civil in nature, and no criminal charges can be invoked.

- Unlike litigation, the parties involved in the arbitration choose the location for the arbitration, whereas, in litigation, the dominion of the courts is decided based on the jurisdiction of the matter.

- ADR is preferred over litigation because it is more cost-effective than litigation. It is a private affair, unlike litigation that proceeds in court.

- It is generally much quicker to resolve an issue.

Arbitration Vs India

Arbitration in India is still in its nascent form. Though all corporate contracts involve an arbitration clause, it still is a lengthy process starting from the appointment of the arbitration tribunal and such issues. There still is a lack of standardised procedures for arbitration which in turn creates a gap in the process and also the outcome. The award by an arbitrator is considered binding, and the process to challenge the same almost does not exist or is too expensive and time-consuming.

The Good News

The good news is, Arbitration laws in India are seeing a remarkable change in recent years. Though settlements have been made through arbitration historically, the trends of globalisation have seen quite a few reforms in the outlook of the government towards arbitration. The recent developments made in the arbitration system help aid the ease of doing business initiative taken up by the government. Keeping in mind that global business houses prefer arbitration over litigation, and they have often been drawing Indian businesses to international arbitrators exposing them to international laws, some reforms have been brought about in the way arbitrations are conducted in India.

- Arbitration settlements now need to be resolved within 12 months of filing with a possible extension of 6 months with express consent from both sides.

- An award given during arbitration may not be stayed by the mere application in a court but only through the due process of pre-admission hearings.

- Arbitration tribunals can now grant interim orders to protect the interest of parties, and such orders would be binding like that of any order passed by the courts.

- Arbitration proceedings can be conducted exclusively on written communication, and oral presentation is optional for the convenience of the parties.

To summarise, Negotiation, Conciliation and Arbitration, now more than ever, have become the route to take for settlement of disputes. There seems to be a change in the acceptance levels of ADR. With this change in the outlook of the society and the governments at large, the art of negotiation, especially as a method of dispute resolution, has become a very important facet in the modern transactional universe.

Chapter 3

Components of Negotiation

Negotiation is undoubtedly the best form of dispute resolution. It is the least expensive, and, if handled well, can be the quickest means to a settlement. Negotiations are a voluntary process and need the will of all parties involved to come to a settlement. The fact that the outcome of a negotiation is not binding on parties is, at times, a positive as the parties involved accept the settlements more openly, and this leaves scope for a better long-term relationship wherever applicable. Negotiations may be done through direct communication or indirect and may be handled as a discussion between parties involved or through a third party. Though there are no set rules for negotiations, there are certain practices that can prove effective in bringing out an easier and more acceptable solution.

Types of Negotiations

Negotiations can be broadly classified into two types: ***Distributive and Integrative***. Distributive type of negotiations mean where parties involved try to maximise their benefit from the outcome. This form of negotiations generally sees a lot of bargaining and jostling for position.

Integrative forms of negotiations are the ones where the parties collectively agree to come together to maximise the benefits for the betterment of the group as a whole. These forms of negotiations would generally see the parties involved in more constructive discussions.

Preparation

Whether negotiating for yourself or as a third party, it is important that you are well prepared. Preparations include understanding the facts of the dispute and also the parties involved. It is important that the negotiator understands all the facts of the issue at hand, the stakes involved and the relationship of parties involved.

In Negotiations, there can be various mindsets involved. Identifying these can make a difference in the methods of approach.

Broadly, mindsets can be classified as the following kinds:

- *Ally*: This group is aligned to your thought process and also stands to benefit from an outcome that you would profess. They would generally tow your line of discussion and would aid your flow of thought being pushed forward.

- *Opposition*: This group does not identify with your approach and may tend to be vary of your propositions. This group might have a natural tendency to counter propositions and object to ideas put forth. This is also the group that needs to be studied and understood the most before entering any negotiation.

- *Fence Sitters*: This group is agonistic and are open to being convinced. The way a negotiator presents an issue to this group becomes key to swinging their vote in his favour.

Understanding data and all the facts of a dispute is key to a negotiation. The build up to any dispute would have communications involved, and at times, promises made and may not be kept. Understanding the circumstances under which these have happened needs to be taken into account before entering into any negotiation. Often, there are inabilities created due to outside factors that may not be in the control for parties to the dispute; understanding such situations also helps as the negotiator can then apply the knowledge to draw more effective and comprehensive solutions.

Relations between parties can often be of mutually dependable nature, and knowing such facts helps in creating a conducive environment for a discussion. The inherent nature of the parties involved also plays an important part in the way discussions are directed. For example, a naturally aggressive side to a discussion will more often than not push their end of the bargain and would try to arm twist the others into submission, and a more subtle side would be more receptive to hearing all sides.

Understanding the market forces involved in a particular dispute, especially in commercial negotiations, is key. For example, the movement of price points and the demand situation of a particular industry can be used as leverage to draw a negotiation to a settlement. This understanding also brings forth a clear scenario of what is at stake and the maximum benefits that can be drawn by each of the parties to a dispute.

A negotiator that follows natural law and logic has a better chance of being accepted. It is a key that negotiators understand the predicaments of all sides involved and what they stand to gain or lose. A settlement that offers a solution considering the above factors generally gets accepted better.

The Process

The process of negotiation itself is dynamic and completely subjective; however, there are certain practices that remain common and can be listed as under:

Understand the Goals

This is the first step of every negotiation, no matter if it is distributive or integrative. A smart negotiator always keeps the goals of all parties involved in perspective so the discussions can be directed to a fruitful conclusion. This helps a negotiator to make offers that can be acceptable to sides even if they are looking at maximising their benefits in a particular deal.

Create Trust

It is important that the negotiator earns the trust of the parties involved. This can be achieved by being transparent and presenting facts on an "as is where is" basis. It is also important that a negotiator is unbiased. At times even the way you are seated during the negotiation gives a feeling of being non biassed. For example, let's look at two sides: 'A' and 'B', who are a party to the negotiation, and in turn they employ 'N' as a neutral negotiator. Here, Party 'A' sits on one side of the table and party 'B' on the other side. In this case, it is imperative that 'N' sits on the head of the table and not on any one side as this very seating itself makes him look unbiased.

Influence Decisions

Through the course of negotiations, it is helpful if the negotiator can pick up markers, which lead to a possible outcome. There can be certain parties that can influence a decision which the negotiator agrees with on either side. These may even be certain issues which give comfort to both parties commonly. If the negotiator is capable of picking up these ques, it can give him a clear vision on the direction the discussion can be steered in.

Specificity

While dealing with facts, make sure that all data is accurately presented on all sides. Errors in presentation of data can be a major reason for failure of a negotiation as it can cause distrust among parties involved. It is also important that data is presented without any bias and should not appear to be presented to create advantage to any side.

Promote Communication

Discussions can be fruitful when all parties get a chance to speak and are heard from. Most disputes arise due to misunderstandings; a system of making one's points and allowing rebuttals helps resolve many of these misgivings. So as far as possible, articulate and to the point communication should be promoted. Even acquisitions made can be allowed if presented in a proper manner, and counters to the same are accommodated.

Keep Away From Emotions

Emotions like anger and sympathy are quite common in such discussions, and one should stay away from these. Articulate and objective analysis of the situation and the possible outcomes can ensure that discussions do not disintegrate and degenerate into chaos.

Keep In Mind The Impact Of The Outcomes

It is important that as negotiations progress, the negotiator considers the impact of the outcome. The more that the negotiations can be driven towards the median, the better. Once discussions are centred around a common ground, it is important that the negotiator leads the discussion more towards an outcome.

Make Concessions Wherever Possible

In a negotiation, it is important that all parties have an intent to solve issues and move ahead. It is also for the negotiator to convince parties to make concessions and allow bargains wherever possible. In issues where the loss or adverse impact is minimum, there must be an effort made to compromise. This leads to better acceptance of remedies.

Keep Moving Forward

Once a certain topic is discussed and agreed upon, it is important that one does not linger on the same. The negotiator needs to ensure that closed issues are not revisited unless it has a bearing on newer issues. If there are points where there is a disagreement that creates an adverse environment, it is advisable to take a break and regroup at a later time.

Create Logs

In case of a long-drawn negotiation with multiple issues, it is advisable to create a log and publish the same to all sides so as to avoid any ambiguity at the end. There can be situations where whole agreements can fall apart due to a misunderstanding in such cases. The logs should be published in the interim stages of such discussion and after every time it is appended. This would help create clarity on all issues addressed and closed.

Arm Twist If Required

At times, a threat or warning of consequence is necessary to bring order to a negotiation. While this is avoidable, it may be used when there is a belief that there is a threat to the progress of the negotiation. This tactic is generally useful in cases of distributive negotiations when certain sides try to take undue advantage of a discussion and may derail the entire negotiation.

Closure and Execution

All outcomes need to be agreed upon by all parties to a negotiation to call it a successful effort. These settlements are generally accepted and executed when there is a consensus among parties, which has been brought about through due process, and when all sides believe that natural justice has prevailed. While negotiation and its outcomes matter, execution of all the measures agreed upon in such deals is the true measure of success. A clear written agreement between all parties helps in creating a sense of responsibility. It is a negotiator's prerogative to step in to help execute the negotiated settlements.

A successful negotiator assesses all the aspects of a dispute before entering into a dispute. A negotiation should ensure that the discussion leads to a non destructive outcome both in the form of value propositions and relations. A smart negotiator is the one who understands the parties, their goals and the prevailing situations and in turn leverages this knowledge to bring disputes to an end. A smart negotiator is also capable of eradicating any bad blood between parties of a dispute and often creates bridges that can be used to maintain working relations in the future.

Chapter 4

Negotiation: A Reality Check

Negotiations are a tricky business. While it is actually just a discussion and statement of facts as a whole, it involves many facets of human psychology. The nature of the relationship of the people involved, the emotional state, and the inherent nature of the people involved in a negotiation play a major role in the way negotiations are conducted and their outcomes.

Let us try and weed out a few *myths* about negotiations in this chapter.

It is assumed that negotiations are just a conversation and the person with the best communication skills generally comes out on top. This is a myth. Most negotiations go far beyond the realm of mere conversations; they involve a complex array of problems. Technical understanding of the subject matter discussed is key in most negotiations, especially commercial negotiations. While the importance of good and effective communication cannot be ignored, an effective negotiator must understand much more. In an effective negotiation, the negotiator has to have a sense of fairness, should understand what is at stake for any of the sides of the negotiation, and should be persuasive enough with a sense of fairness and a bias to natural law and justice. Effective negotiation is where all parties feel that they have been given a fair deal, and to make this happen, the negotiator needs to have a few aspects under control before and during the actual process.

Understanding Facts

A well-prepared negotiator understands the nuances of the type of dispute being resolved; he understands the technicalities of the issue and also the acceptable legal precedent. In case of commercial or business disputes, he needs to understand unsaid industry practices and rituals. A well-informed negotiator will be better equipped to drive talks in the right direction, pivot when required, and also come up with effective suggestions that are generally more acceptable.

Understand the Stakes

Understanding what is at stake and what it means to each side is very important for a negotiator. For example, the side with more to lose is usually more open to an amicable outcome. A party that stands to gain much also has the same attitude. This understanding of the parties involved would help in placing the right deals on the table and deciding on the kind of concessions that should be given to take discussions towards closure.

Data Is Everything

Well, maybe not, but it is a very important factor. Having accurate information backed by precise data helps the discussions and also establishes credibility for the negotiator. Before any negotiation, it is imperative that the negotiator looks at and authenticates all the facts of the matter. Checking the last document involved often helps reveal solutions even before the actual process of negotiations begins.

Create Credibility

When the process of negotiation starts, it is important that a negotiator or a mediator creates his or her own credibility for the group. A sense of fairness is important for all parties to be open to suggestions made. The process of negotiation, unlike litigation, is a process of communication, where the negotiator often plays a moderator's role. It is his job to make sure that the talks are directed to the relevant subjects and emotions are kept in check.

Know When to Close

This is the key part of any negotiation. While discussions can go on and push and pulls could take forever, a smart negotiator knows when to make an offer and take discussions to a closure. This, however, is easier said than done. All the factors that we discussed above bring the negotiator to this judgement. A smart negotiator often drives the discussion to this point so that the offer becomes inevitable. It is also important to keep in mind that settlements that are accepted by all sides more openly have a better chance of being executed and not challenged later.

So to summarise, negotiation is not just effective communication and endless banter; it has a lot more elements to it, and a master negotiator would subjugate all the ingredients and probably a bit more.

Negotiation can be Handled Only by Lawyers

Historically, negotiations in the business world were always handled by lawyers and their law firms. This was based on the fact that lawyers understood the legal system well, and any outcome of negotiations that involved them would be close to the most acceptable legal principle. However, as the world of business has evolved, the transactional intricacies have changed too. The world now is very dynamic, and the implication of any transaction is not just legal but has many other facets to it. The change in the way technology has stepped into our lives, and the way financial transactions have evolved has made negotiations more complex and multifaceted for just a lawyer or a law firm to handle.

There is a marked change in the way that even courts now look at mediation. In the wake of the new world, the courts have stepped up globally and have now encouraged the conflicting parties to look at expertise beyond just lawyers to look at negotiating settlements.

So, to think that the world of negotiations just revolves around legal experts settling issues is now a myth.

Historically, people of influence and individuals of repute were always looked up to and were invited to negotiate settlements; the stature and the sense of fairness, which they brought to the table, helped in settling many disputes. The modern world is actually now looking at professionals from various walks of life to step into this role. This is often to do with their expertise in the particular field. For example, disputes between technology companies on matters like IP are best sorted by a negotiator who understands the subject and can communicate efficiently on issues related to technology.

There are cases where third parties from the same industry and often even competition have stepped in to resolve issues as the resolution was best for their industry as a whole.

Negotiations are a Waste of Time

The next thought that is doing the rounds is that negotiations are a waste of time, and since outcomes of litigation are binding, it is a better route to take.

False,

Why?

Cause litigation is also time-consuming and can be challenged as well. While litigation is totally based on hearing a case on both sides and based on evidence provided, there is an award made. In Negotiation, there is essentially a winner and a loser. Even the winner, in this case, may be unhappy with what has been offered and can still go ahead to challenge the decision in a higher court and so on and so forth. In case of litigation, the award is passed as a judgement, and the acceptability of the award to any of the sides is not considered.

This is where negotiation differs

First of all, negotiations are attended voluntarily and are a platform for all parties involved to have an open discussion.

- This discussion not only looks at pieces of evidence and facts but also the human angles are involved too. It considers the impact of an outcome on the negotiations for all the sides involved.

- Negotiators believe that a settlement with complete acceptance would bring about better chances of execution on all sides and hence proposes win-win solutions.

- Though outcomes of negotiations can be challenged, they seldom are as the agreements are arrived at on mutual consent.

- Negotiations are a more private affair, and unlike litigation, they don't tend to have an open impact on the image of the parties involved.

- It is certainly more convenient as the time and place of these discussions are agreed upon per the convenience of those involved.

- It is certainly less expensive as it does not involve paying fees, bonds, etc.

Negotiations, hence prove to be more effective than litigation in most cases.

The next aspect to be considered is What are the chances of a win in negotiations?

To begin with, the chances of a win in litigation are quite simply based on the pieces of evidence and, more often than not, on who has a better lawyer. Negotiations approach a dispute more by getting into a win-win angle than through a one-sided approach.

So it is safe to assume that losing in a negotiation is difficult. Negotiations are generally a more considerate affair, and there are many times concessions given to all sides to create comfort in the outcome.

So while we really cannot predict what the outcome of litigation might be, it is safe to assume that the outcome of a negotiation is mostly not a loss.

Won't Negotiation be an Ego Battle?

Disagreements of any kind and resolutions thereof can always be made into an egoistic affair, so to think that negotiations would be the only platform to bring that to the fore would be a wrong notion. If you come to think of the way each of these functions, negotiations help a dialogue and bridge gaps better than any other mode of resolution.

The one other thing that needs to be considered is that negotiations, due to the sheer nature of being more communicative, help in ensuring better relationships, even in cases where there are bitter disputes.

To summarise, Negotiation is based on relationships, understanding of the industry and the nuances of a particular issue, and natural law from a human angle. It is safe to assume that this is the most cost-effective and the least destructive tool for a resolution.

Chapter 5

Impact of Culture on Negotiations

The cultural framework of a society influences the acceptance of negotiations. A less aggressive community is more prone to accept negotiations as a mode of settlement. A very interesting study made in the animal kingdom can be a great example of this view. According to research, humans have a 99.5% DNA match to the chimpanzee; the chimpanzee world is full of violence, may it be for mating rights or territory. There is a hierarchical system, which is maybe as complex as human society. The formation of alliances and domination is a part of the social structure, and conflicts are a regular part of the chimp society. While in the chimp society, most disputes are settled by battle and submission by one party, another cousin of the chimp, the bonobo, has a very different approach to life. The bonobo society is peaceful and almost conflict-free. The disputes here are settled more by the common good. Bonds between the primates in a group are very strong, and they believe in an equitable distribution of resources. In some cases, these primates are also known to adopt orphaned babies of their kind and raise them. This points to the fact that the design of society with reference to their culture has a huge impact on the acceptance of negotiation as a tool to settle disputes.

If we look at human civilization as a whole, historically, certain parts of the world are certainly more disturbed than others. The conflicted nature of regions is very evident and long-standing; disputes may be based on religious divides or on the basis of rights to resources. There is also a direct correlation between a culture's attitude toward peaceful negotiations and the development of human life and value. The biggest example is the war-torn regions in Africa, where there is hardly any improvement in the quality of life of people, in direct contrast to the Scandinavian countries that seem to enjoy a better happiness index.

As the world grows smaller and technology pushes us to a further globalised world, with every society being dependent on each other and every action of a society having an impact on everyone else, this cultural aspect of humans comes to the fore more prominently. An example of this is the armed conflict between Russia and Ukraine. Here, dialogues have failed and the adversities have an impact far more expansive than just the countries involved. This region exports about one-third of the world's wheat and almost the same amount of sunflower and maize oil to the world. The blockade of the port in BlackSea has resulted in a drop in supplies worldwide, pushing up food prices globally.

Furthermore, various factors influence the way a society behaves.

Education

Generally, a better-educated society is believed to be more accepting and open to discussions and negotiations on matters. The main reason for this is believed to be the open understanding of the cause and effects of a dispute. Better educated societies are also more aware of the background of the opposing side(s), and at most times, this empathy helps in a more conducive environment for discussion.

Financial Well-Being

A society that has more to lose is often more inclined to be peaceful. It is often seen that the conflicts are higher in poorer societies, and there is much lesser scope for discussion. This is probably due to the fact that when there is much to lose, individuals and the community, as a whole, are more conscious of the approach that they take.

Faith and Beliefs

Our faith and our belief systems also have a huge impact on us as a society. Belief systems that make us feel superior and entitled lead us to confrontations, especially in cases where the opposing side does not share the same faith. Holy wars have plagued humanity for almost ever. Societies that tend to believe in more hard-line ideologies are less open to a resolution of disputes through less aggressive means.

Geographical Impact

Where you are on the globe also has a say in how you behave as a community. The more blessed the region as far as natural resources are concerned, the more peaceful the society. This may also have something to do with what society has to lose in case of a conflict; hence, they need to be measured in their approach.

Geo-Political Influence

It is also often seen that cultures that are inherently believed to behave in a certain manner change their approach based on the geopolitical influences on them as a society. The approach of neighbouring countries or the change in behaviour of a particular group of countries that share similar values can bring about a change in the way a certain society behaves.

Indian Culture and its Influence on Indian acceptance of Negotiation as a medium of Settlement

India, owing to its rich cultural heritage, has put much faith in the concept of Dharma. Dharma, contrary to the popular belief, stands separate from religion. It means duty, and we also believe in Karma or one's doings, which we believe gives us an outcome that was to be in lieu of the same. This belief system has helped us as a society to be more accepting and pious in our approach towards the world. The Sanskrit words "Lokah Samastah Sukinho Bhavantu" comprise one of the most popular chants, when translated into English, the words mean- May All Beings Everywhere Be Happy and Free, a sentiment we can certainly all relate to wanting ultimately the whole world to be peaceful. This has impetuously led us to be one of the most tolerant societies.

The sub-continent practiced the culture of negotiations through Rajdoots or diplomats before every war. A messenger was sent to the opposing side, and messages from the kings were exchanged as a method to settle issues before every battle. Strategic decision-making was warranted as a part of the Raj-dharma of every king, and it was needed of him to save the lives of his soldiers and avoid war in whatever way possible. In South India, disputes were even settled by two warriors from each side fighting to the death so that a huge blood bath could be prevented. There was always consideration given to the best possible approach to settling a dispute without armed conflict.

The Modern India that emerged post the long struggle for independence has maintained this civil stance. As a country, India has ensured that a dialogue preludes any conflict and, at many junctures, accepted a settlement even in cases where it had a clear advantage by pushing forth the conflict.

The Simla Agreement entered between India and Pakistan after the 1971 war is a great example of how India, even though it had an advantage over its enemy, agreed to a settlement and entered into a peace treaty without making any claims to any of the geographical areas of its neighbour and even returned the 93000 POWs that it had captured. Before this, the Indus water treaty is also a great example of how India agreed to share the water resources with its neighbours on a fair basis of population distribution and also has upheld that treaty despite many fallouts between the two sides in recent years.

India has also played a major role in trying to negotiate a peace pact between the Sri Lankan Government and the rebel Tamil group and, to a great extent, was successful in bridging the divide. It also played a major role in providing humanitarian aid in the region and tried to hold up human rights in the region to a great degree of success.

The civil society in India, as diverse as it is, has also had many junctures where its integrity was tested. We as a society came out on the right side, aided only by our accommodative attitude. Post-partition, riots had almost decimated the country, and where the minorities that were in Pakistan saw persecution and second-grade treatment, the administration and the people of our country ensured peace and acceptance. While minorities that stayed back in Pakistan lost all their belongings, including their faith, minorities here were treated with dignity and their rights upheld. This stemmed from the fact that the society in this country was more accepting and willing to negotiate and give concessions on human grounds for the greater good.

The way our constitution is framed also shows the care that we have taken to be as inclusive as we can in the way we conduct our lives. Though inspired by the established democracies of America and Britain, our forefathers were careful enough to ensure that every member of the society was given a voice and also heard. The linguistic separation of the country later is also another great example of how we managed to stay together despite disagreements. The states came into being with barely a skirmish as we drew lines to make administration easier.

The greatest negotiation in the history of the country, however, might have been the expression of the state of Kashmir. This negotiation happened when there was a battle raging, and Kashmir as a state was vulnerable to being overrun. India had a clear advantage as the then King of Kashmir would have agreed to any condition that India would have put forth. But even then, the country chose to be as giving as it could, and this new state was given special status as demanded by the erstwhile monarch.

This attitude of the majority of people in India gives hope to the fact that negotiations will take root as the most used method of negotiations in India. The challenges await India and would probably test us as a society.

Proposal for a Common Civil Code: This was a clause that was a part of the directive principle of the Constitution and has been a part of the current government's agenda. With various ideas and religions and beliefs and faiths, this might be the most difficult chapter in the way we communicate with each other. Codifying various laws and making them acceptable to all will be a challenge that will polarise us. How we negotiate this chapter in our history will have a lot to say about us as a people.

Changed Immigration Laws: The NRC, which has been a hot topic of disagreement, though yet to be formalised, will see the country divided in its ideologies. While this is a reality in most countries, we, as a society, have had our disagreements on the issue, and we will need to find an acceptable way to implement this as a national policy. Whether we achieve this with consensus or if battle lines will be drawn is yet to be seen.

The Settlement of Issues with the Naxalites: While the world's attention has been on Kashmir and the terrorism that plagues the region, a big issue that plagues the western and central regions of the nation is the Maoist Naxalite movement. How the government and we as a society as a whole deal with this crisis and bring the brethren back into mainstream social life is going to be a crucial negotiation

Winds of Change

While the judicial system has been over-burdened and civil disputes almost take forever to be resolved, there seems to be a monumental change in the approach of society, and more so of business towards the settlement of disputes. More and more professionals like lawyers and CAs are looking at being qualified negotiators, and business houses are now looking to hire mediators to settle disputes instead of lawyers. The development in IT architecture also is making life easier for such negotiations to happen. There is no more a constraint of geographical distances or of time and venues to meet. Online platforms are now facilitating meetings and negotiations from drawing rooms of houses. Even international business negotiations have moved beyond these constraints.

There is also a new point of view of law firm practice, which does not thrive on conflict but on the resolution of conflict. Private third-party negotiators who have come up with tech platforms to ensure easy, cost-effective dispute resolution will now lead dispute resolution into a new era. Unlike the traditional-typical law firms, the interest of these firms does not lie in long-drawn litigation but in quick and acceptable resolutions. These firms are now taking up positions as virtual legal departments for companies that help them draw up contracts, help in due diligence, and enter new business alliances. This hand-holding continues in cases of disputes, and these firms even manage to hire professionals with the technical expertise to help clients in their relevant fields of business.

The time we can believe is not far when law firms will be replaced by firms that will now become business partners to companies and start helping them resolve disputes, letting them focus on their core competencies.

Chapter 6

PrivateCourt – The Emergence

Negotiations are often considered to be a reactive process where a negotiator often has a loosely built approach and then responds to how the other side behaves. This might be only partially true. Though negotiations are reactive in many cases, there is a lot of preparation that goes into planning a strategy in your approach. Many factors need to be considered and a clear strategy planned right from the onset for the desired outcome is key. While we have discussed all the steps that need to be taken to ensure a clean and positive negotiation, some specifics go into preparing that a specialised team undertakes.

Fact Check

Checking all facts of a dispute and the claims made by either side needs to be analysed in detail. One missed point may prove disastrous to the process and may derail the entire effort. Also, checking on the accuracy of the data presented cannot be over-emphasised. This collation of facts with the legal precedence for the same needs to be looked at as one prepares for a discussion. The facts that are presented also need to be accepted by all parties, and all communication that is presented needs to be acknowledged by all sides. This is to say that assumptions need to be avoided, and only clean and clear data that is Non-ambiguous needs to be presented.

Plan For Outcomes

Negotiation is a dynamic affair, and outcomes are often determined by the will of all the parties that are involved. While the best outcomes for negotiation are desired, a negotiator also needs to be prepared with alternate plans. The negotiator needs to be clear on the bottom line that is acceptable to the party represented and should have the agreement of the party to settle on the same in case the scenario presents itself. This also means that the team needs to preempt all possible oppositions that it may face during the negotiation and also decide on points of pivot that may need to be taken as the discussions carry on. These might need to be considered in advance, and approvals from the client need to be taken as there may not be a time during the negotiations to do the same. The team, through its brainstorming sessions, comes up with all such points and discusses the same with its clients well in advance so clarity on the same can be achieved

Ancillary Facts

A negotiator needs to be aware of the other factors that would influence the process. These may be market sentiments, competitors, etc. These factors would determine the response of the parties to any negotiation. Favourable factors may also be used as leverage to drive negotiations into favourable corners.

Ensuring Execution

While negotiations might end on an acceptance of settlement, the negotiator's role does not end there. Ensuring compliance with the agreement is also a part of the process. While a sign-off on the agreement is done, the negotiator needs to gauge the willingness of the parties to honour their side of the bargain. While this is not an exact science, skilled negotiators can fathom the intent through body language and such subtle signs that the process comes to a close on.

While the world is moving towards using professional negotiators to settle disputes quickly and amicably, companies are coming up with the idea to start such ventures. PrivateCourt stemmed from this very thought of providing professional negotiations and mediation services to business houses in India.

With businesses moving to tech platforms and startups sprouting everywhere, a venture like this would surely add value. The company now undertakes negotiation services and mediation services for every industry.

Envisaged as a partner to business houses, PrivateCourt looks at helping its clients cut time and maximise results in any negotiation or mediation/ dispute resolution. A team of highly skilled individuals, who come from the field of law, commerce, and technology, has come together to make the process of business negotiations.

The team is dedicated and process-oriented when it comes to any negotiation, notwithstanding the industry or the size of the stakes. The team works as an extended team for the clients and digs deep to make sure that the best results can be arrived at.

At PrivateCourt, any dispute negotiation is broken down into steps, and information is logged to ensure complete preparedness before and after the discussions happen.

The process involves the following main stages:

Understanding the Dispute

This is probably the most important part of the process as this sets the tone for all that is to follow. An assigned process lead is the key person involved in this bit; this person is also entrusted with facilitating all the factors that need to come together for a successful negotiation. Understanding the issue at hand and creating a log of the case is the first step of the process. The lead also ensures that the log is read and understood by the client or its representatives so that the same can be put forth for preparation.

Verification

To ensure that all aspects of a case are looked at, a team of relevant individuals looks at all documents filed and all communications made available. This is also the juncture at which the accuracy of data and its match to the claim is verified. Any missing documents or additional documents are flagged, and then a request to furnish the same is raised with the client. In case of any anomalies, an explanation is sought, or corrections to the claim itself are suggested. The legal compatibility of all documents submitted is also checked and cleared. This is probably one of the most important parts of a negotiation as it also helps to decide the approach that needs to be taken and the probable rebuttals that will be put forth by the opposing side.

Expert Views

Depending on the industry and the skill levels required to handle said negotiations, subject matter experts (SMEs) are assigned, and inputs from them are incorporated into the draft plan of action. The team ensures that all standard compliances are met and industry practices are aligned in this phase. Parallel to this, the market review team collects market information on a broad spectrum, including any specific detail, if required by the opposing party, is assimilated into the information. The opinions of the SMEs are logged and made available for discussions that will aid to come up with a plan of action to be followed during the negotiation process.

Pre Negotiation Plans

The team, along with the lead negotiator, now enters into a preparation phase. This involves all the information collected and tabulated, read with the inputs given by the subject matter expert. All possible objections that may come up during negotiations are also discussed during this phase, and rebuttals are prepared and agreed upon. Once all these are placed on board, a possible outcome is established. The deviations to the plan and a worst-case scenario are also played out with agreed outcomes.

Negotiation Phase

This is where all the preparations come together; the assigned mediator initiates negations and presents data. Efforts are also taken by the mediator to direct the conversations toward desired goals. He might pivot basis the information exchanged or counter arguments presented at all times, maintaining the equilibrium of the discussion, never once ignoring the human angle to it. It is critical that all parties in the discussions feel that they have been heard and their contentions addressed.

Execution Phase

The mediator's job does not end with just getting the parties to agree to a settlement but also continues till the said agreement has been executed by all sides. As a company, there is a team assigned to ensure that the timelines and agreed terms are met as per schedule. The constant follow-up by the team helps persuade parties to the agreement to honour their side of the bargain.

PrivateCourt understands that any dispute that lingers for a long time takes a lot out of business. Resolution through litigation is expensive and time-consuming, which pushes businesses further into losses. The greatest loss, we believe, is the loss of man-hours, which otherwise can be put into more productive activities that are consumed by the disputes. The vision of PrivateCourt is to act as an agency to its clients and make sure that time and efforts taken to resolve an issue are kept to the minimum.

Another fact that needs to be considered, especially in business litigation, is that in most cases, disputes occur between a company and its customers. A typically legal solution often misses this fact, and at times, a victory in litigation ends up as a loss as you probably lose a customer. PrivateCourt believes in the human approach to justice and advocates compromise in the short term to make a long-term gain. Wherever there is a will to continue business relations, the option should be taken, and PrivateCourt recognises this fact and advocates resolutions that are a win-win for all sides involved.

While a dispute begins, all parties have a certain set of approaches and desired results that they chase. PrivateCourt owing to the experience and exposure to different case scenarios and multiple businesses has the capability to bring a fresh perspective to a debate- "out of the box solutions", as you may call them. Every business runs on what they call industry practices, and often a resolution or a way out taken in case of one industry may fit the other with certain tweaks. The fact that PrivateCourt deals with various industries and can cross reference such solutions can often prove to be very effective.

To summarise, PrivateCourt is a company set up with the sole aim of helping businesses large and small to navigate their business negotiations effectively and quickly. The aim is to become a business partner who takes care of all negotiations internally or externally so that the efforts of the business can remain focused on its own core competencies.

Case Studies

We can now look at some case studies that will show how the use of a professional team can add value to any business house. This will also throw light on how the various steps taken by PrivateCourt bring about a new perspective to negotiations.

Case Study 1

Post Production Studio Vs. Entertainment Company

Claim Raised on: 08/06/2021

Conciliation Date: 25/06/2021

Settlement Date:25/06/2021

Digest: Mediation/Conciliation/Dispute/Claimant/ Respondent/Invoice/Settlement

Case Summary

In July of 2021, **PrivateCourt** was approached by a movie studio, referred to herein as the Claimant, in Mumbai, to negotiate a dispute arising out of nonpayment of invoice by an entertainment company referred to herein as the Respondent. The claimant providing post-production and private screening of movies as one of its services, was engaged by the respondent to provide movie screenings for its special audience and review panels for their upcoming release. The movie studio was also requested to hold a small after party with food and beverages for the guests at the theatre. Three such screenings were scheduled to be held over a period of 2 weeks.

It is apparently common practice in the movie industry where a private movie theatre is hired to have small releases to audiences who have a positive impact on the marketing of the film.

Also, there is no practice of any formal agreement signed.

The Issue

While there was absolute clarity on the rentals to be paid for the screening of the movie, there remained ambiguity in the invoice amount quoted for the after-party event. Since the claimant was not in the business of catering to such after-party events, a third-party vendor was hired by the claimant to cater to the after-party request.

The claimant raised two invoices: one for the studio rentals and the other for the hospitality charges. **While the studio rentals were duly accepted and paid for, a major dispute arose to settle the invoices raised for the party hosted.**

Our chief negotiator in this case, along with his team, assessed all communications submitted by both parties as evidence: Ledger accounts, Outstanding invoices, Email conversations, Purchase Orders, and Whatsapp chats. The team also had to closely review all the interaction material submitted as evidence that the claimant had with the third-party vendor **and made a big discovery.** While the disputed invoice amount for the after party was quoted as Rs. 2,68,020/- by the vendor, the team realised that the claimant was overcharged by the vendor. The claimant then got a revised invoice after pointing out this fact to the vendor.

The respondent was then approached with a corrected invoice amount of Rs. 1,00,000/- (rounded down for convenience). The respondent reacted with a bit of resistance and reluctance to accept due to his earlier experience and was unsure of the accuracy of the invoice amount.

The negotiator, owing to his experience and expertise, ironed out all doubts that were raised on the respondent's end, explained the details and a settlement was agreed upon.

The Negotiation

The respondent agreed to pay the outstanding amount of Rs. 1,00,000/- by a bank transfer to the Claimant's bank account in two equal instalments.

- The first instalment of Rs. 50,000/- the very next working day dating 26/06/2021.

- The second instalment of Rs. 50,000/- in the subsequent 20 days dating to 17/07/2021.

The Inference

This case is peculiar as the negotiator also became an auditor and saved both the claimant and the respondent a large chunk of money. This also helped in holding up the reputation of the claimant and ensured continual business from his client.

Case Study 2

Digital Marketing Company Vs. Online Apparel Brand

Date of Claim raised:15/02/2022

Date of Conciliation: 23/02/2022

Date of Settlement: 16/02/2022

Digest: Mediation/Conciliation/Dispute/Claimant/ Respondent/Invoice/Settlement

Case Summary

This was a dispute that came up between a digital marketing company based in Mumbai and a Delhi based online apparel brand. While the digital marketing company (Claimant) was into the business of brand promotions and the online apparel brand (respondent) were an online startup into the business of selling customised T-shirts online. Being a typical startup the apparel brand needed to have a good online presence and needed the help of the digital marketing company to help them with the same. The digital marketing company was hired to create online properties and to increase website traffic. This was a long term engagement and was to be a continuous process for a period of one year. The claimant was supposed to raise invoices for all the separate activities and there would be a rolling credit of 15 days for each invoice. The dispute occurred after 3 months of the project when the respondent started delaying payments of invoices raised.

The issue

The respondent, being a startup, was in the market looking for funding and had started the activity based on certain promises of funds coming through. Though they were making good headway in developing an online market for their product, they were not able to secure the first round of funding on time. Though they had the funds to support the operations, they now decided to divert it towards order fulfilment and creation of further stockpiles and ignored the payments to be made to the Claimant. As the digital marketing activities were a constant process, the receivables mounted to a sum of Rs. 5,49,000/-. The claimant approached PrivateCourt to negotiate for settlement.

The Process

The Negotiator looked through all the documentation and established the credibility of the claim. Once he was satisfied with the accuracy, a discussion with the respondent was initiated. Understanding the issues of fund flow at the respondent's end, the negotiator also explained how the activities conducted by the claimant were important for the online business to continue on the right path. The negotiator also explained that the online property that was built over the past few months would drop in value if the activities were discontinued. Realising the problem at hand, the respondent asked for deferred payment options for the accrued invoices and also promised to pay any new invoices basis the originally agreed terms. The request was run through with the claimant, and a settlement was arrived upon.

Terms of Settlement

The respondent would settle the accrued invoices in 5 equal parts of Rs. 1,09,800/- paid within the 15th of every calendar month. Failing to do this would prompt an immediate stop to all activities conducted by the claimant and there would be an 18% p.a. penalty charged on all outstanding amounts.

- The first payment, amounting to Rs. 1,09,800/- on or before 15/03/2022.

- The second payment, amounting to Rs. 1,09,800/-on or before 15/04/2022.

- The third payment, amounting to Rs. 1,09,800/- on or before 15/05/2022.

- The fourth payment, amounting to Rs. 1,09,800/- on or before 15/06/2022.

- The fifth payment, amounting to Rs. 1,09,800/- on or before 15/07/2022.

The Inference

Though there was a delay in payment, the negotiator, in this case, was not only able to get the settlement but also ensure that both parties continued their business relationship.

Case Study 3

Digital Marketing Company Vs Tech Start-up

Date of Claim raised:15/01/2022

Date of Conciliation: 22/01/2022

Date of Settlement: 21/02/2022

Case Summary

The dispute was between a technology company providing Digital Marketing services and a Tech startup in the e-learning arena. The tech startup (Respondent) hired the technology company (Claimant) for providing digital marketing services. The digital marketing company was to provide end-to-end marketing solutions, including SEO/SEM services, website content management, and lead generation. Both parties being based out of Bangalore, many meetings were held in person and, at times, sparsely documented. Payments for lead generation services were to be made in advance, but other marketing activities needed to be billed every month. While the respondent made payments for the lead generation activity, invoices raised for the other marketing activities were partially paid. On being approached, the argument given was that they needed to see the impact of the activities over a period of time to decide the effectiveness.

The Issue

The bone of contention was that the cost of marketing, which was borne by the claimant, had to be settled by the respondent in 30-day cycles as it would help the activity to be continued. The delay in payment not only meant that the respondent lost money but also meant that the activities could not be continued, and the online properties that were developed started losing their positioning. While the respondent kept paying for the lead generation activity and was satisfied with the results thereof.

The Process

The negotiator established the claims after an in-depth review of the evidence and documentation submitted by both parties. These included email communications, WhatsApp chats, invoice records, minuted meeting records, etc. Once the claim was established, the Negotiator then had a detailed discussion with the respondent on how the nonpayment was affecting not only the claimant but also the activities that were being conducted online for his business as well. The respondent was also informed that the nonpayment of dues would result in the claimant forfeiting the amount paid towards lead generation activity, and that would also compound the troubles for the respondent. An amicable settlement needed to be reached for the outstanding amount of Rs. 10,50,000/, and the same was agreed by the respondent.

Terms of Settlement

The Respondent agreed to pay the settled amount of Rs. 10,50,000/- to the Claimant as per the below-mentioned schedule:

- The first payment, amounting to Rs. 4,00,000/-on or before 07/03/2022.

- The second payment, amounting to Rs. 2,25,000/- on or before 07/04/2022.

- The third payment, amounting to Rs. 2,25,000/-on or before 01/05/2022.

- The fourth payment, amounting to Rs. 2,00,000/-on or before 31/05/2022.

The Inference

The Negotiator's ability to explain the lose-lose scenario to the respondent brought about a quick resolution and also ensured continuity of business for both parties.

Case Study 4

Textile Manufacturer Vs. Wholesaler of Textile

Cast Number PVTCRT/CD/150

Claim raised on: 22/06/2021

Conciliation Date: 06/08/2021

Digest: Mediation/Conciliation/Dispute/Claimant/Respondent/Invoice/Settlement

Case Summary

Financial disputes need to be resolved as quickly as possible. The claimant (a Private Limited Company engaged in manufacturing of Textile Business) claimed Rs. 1,01,478/- owed by the defendant (a wholesaler of Textiles) for failure to pay an outstanding invoice with respect to the textile materials supplied.

The defendant contended that the invoice was incorrect and that he was willing to pay a percentage of the bill, which he felt was valid. The defendant discerned that the remainder should be waived as he was given verbal assurance by the claimant that costs would be kept to a minimum contrary to which he was being billed for, a large amount he felt he could have gotten supplied at a discounted rate through another vendor.

The Issue/Dispute/Argument/Claim/Discourse/ Disagreement/Scenario

Through the negotiations, both the parties had a chance to put their points across. The claimant put forth that there was constant communication, though verbal, regarding the price changes of raw materials and the effect of the same on the cost of finished products. He also acclaimed that maybe a small percentage could have been reduced by alternate sourcing of goods. This, however, was not possible due to the short delivery time expected by the respondent.

The respondent inturn came back with some alternate quotes received from other vendors at prices that were much lower than the ones given by the claimant.

The Negotiator, Mr. Ankit Verma, first carefully scrutinised details submitted by both parties, which included the following: Ledger accounts, Outstanding invoices, Email conversations, Purchase Orders, and Whatsapp chats.

He then reviewed the price tabs of raw materials quoted at the time of the order being furnished and brought to the notice of the respondent that the same are not comparable as there was a steep fall in the prices later. The documentary evidence provided by the negotiator was a convincing explanation.

The Process/Undertaking/Action

The negotiator, in this case, had to listen to arguments from both sides, and the pain points of both sides were listed. Documentary evidence, including third-party quotes from other vendors, was examined to understand where the respondent's assessment of cost came from. The negotiator had to indulge in a bit of research to establish cost differences during the time elapsed between the order processing and this day.

The Settlement Agreement

The respondent agreed to the claim, and the case was settled on 06/02/2022.

The outstanding amount of Rs. 1,01,478/- to be transferred via a bank transfer to the Claimant's bank account on or before February 2022.

The schedule of payment is as below:

- 30/08/2021- Rs. 15,000/-
- 30/09/2021- Rs. 15,000/-
- 30/10/2021- Rs. 15,000/-
- 30/11/2021- Rs. 15,000/-
- 30/12/2021- Rs. 15,000/-
- 30/01/2022- Rs. 15,000/-
- 28/02/2022- Rs. 11,478/-

The Inference

Differences of opinion may occur due to certain misconstrued market information. Negotiation, in this case, helps by bringing perspective to the disconnect and, at times, explaining actions to either party.

Case Study 05

NBFC vs Trading Company

Date of Claim raised:15/02/2022

Date of Conciliation: 10/03/2022

Date of Settlement: 16/04/2022

Digest: Mediation/Conciliation/Dispute/Claimant/ Respondent/Invoice/Settlement

Case Summary

This dispute arose between a trading company and an NBFC, both based in Uttar Pradesh. The Claimant is an NBFC in the business of providing packing credit and bill discounting services to SMEs. The Respondent is a trading company, which is in the business of distribution of sodium bicarbonate to plastic product manufacturers in the north of India. The respondent had borrowed an amount of Rs. 1,63,000/- from the claimant for a consignment imported against a purchase order of Rs. 2,86,000/-. While the credit was given for a period of 90 days, the respondent failed to pay back, stating reasons for non-receipt of payments from his buyer. Courtesy of another 30 days extension was given by the claimant, which again was breached.

The Issue

The claimant, in good faith, had agreed not to levy any extra penal interest for the credit line extension for 30 days. Despite this gesture, the respondent did not make good on his promise and defaulted further with only a part payment of Rs. 30,000/- with a further request for an extension, with no clear date of closure.

The Claimant approached PrivateCourt for settlement.

The Process

The negotiator, in this case, went through all agreed terms and conditions between the parties and concluded that the respondent had indeed overshot all deadlines of payment and did not have a clear plan of repaying his debts. The loan being unsecured had also aided in his complacency. The negotiator, in his conversation with the respondent, made it clear to him that there could be an impact on his credit scores in the future, and the claimant could inform his other creditors, where he enjoyed credit limits, to make his account substandard. This, in the long run, would affect his ability to procure any credits from the market, which is essential in his line of business. The respondent was asked to settle the amount in full, which he agreed to.

The Settlement Terms

The following terms were agreed:

The respondent to pay the remainder i.e. Rs. 1,33,000/- of the amount in two equal instalments of Rs. 66,500/- each on 16th March 2022 and on 16th April 2022 respectively.

The Inference

At times, effectively communicating the ill-effects of payment default to respondents with legal and business precedent helps settle issues effectively and quickly.

Case Study 06

Chemical Manufacturer Vs Trader

Date of Claim raised:01/09/2021

Date of Conciliation: 20/09/2021

Date of Settlement: 20/09/2021

Digest: Mediation/Conciliation/Dispute/Claimant/ Respondent/Invoice/Settlement

Case Summary

This dispute was between a chemical manufacturing company based in Madhya Pradesh as the Claimant and a trader based in Gujarat as the Respondent. While claimant had supplied materials of a specific dye type to the respondent as they had a working relationship with each other over the past few years, the materials were supplied on a 90-day credit term. The dispute came up when a part of the payment amounting to Rs. 3,09,419/- was not paid even post the credit period.

The Issue

The deal was that the claimant would supply the chemicals of specific specs to the respondent, the order was placed with the purchase order with the particulars and the quantity to be supplied. While the claimant had supplied the materials within the stipulated time period, the respondent denied part of this payment, citing reasons that the specifications to certain parts of the order were not met. Despite several rounds of discussions between the parties, there was no head way, and Private Court was entrusted with the mediation.

The Process

The Mediator studied the documents and established the authenticity of the claim. While discussing the issue with the respondent, what came forth was that the team had overlooked a small nuance in the order, which actually was a clerical error from the side of the respondent in the order form. Somehow, in the whole deal, both the sides had missed out on checking the same, and this, as established by the Mediator, proved that the goods supplied were up to standards, and the onus now lay on the respondent to honour the deal. However, this error also created a loss for the business on the respondent's side as he could not supply the materials further ahead. Considering these facts, an extended deferred payment term was granted on mutual agreement.

The Settlement Agreement

The Respondent agreed to pay the outstanding amount of Rs. 3,09,419/- by a bank transfer, to be paid on or before April 2022, in 8 monthly instalments.

The Inference

A trained eye of a professional can bring forth what many times people miss in the heat of arguments.

Case Study 07

Digital Marketing Company Vs Infotech Company

Date of Claim raised: 05/11/2021

Date of Conciliation: 18/11/2021

Date of Settlement: 18/11/2021

Digest: Mediation/Conciliation/Dispute/Claimant/ Respondent/Invoice/Settlement

Case Summary

The case is about a disagreement between a company in the business of Digital Marketing Solutions based in Bangalore and an Infotech company based in Delhi. The claimant, in this case, the Digital Marketing solution provider, was approached by the IT company to create a 3D model walk through of an upcoming apartment complex for one of its clients. The project was to be delivered for a Virtual Reality platform, which would enable prospective buyers to have a feel of the final property once constructed. The delivery time for this project was 120 days. While there was an advance demanded, the claimant agreed to being paid on the completion of the project at the request of the respondent. The project was delivered within the stipulated time period, but the respondent did not honour his payment promises.

The Issue

While the project was delivered and the clients had signed off on the acceptance letter, they did not honour the pay on delivery commitment. The issue occurred as their client in turn had got a quote from one of their competitors and had purchased the said walk through from them without informing or cancelling the order placed with the respondent. Now that the product had been delivered, the respondent was in a fix as its clients denied payment, leading to an outstanding amount of Rs. 7,88,279/-. After much debate between the two parties, PrivateCourt was asked to take up the matter for settlement.

The Process

While the Mediator went through all the documents, the legitimacy of the claim was established and a discussion was initiated. While the mediator heard and understood the predicament, the suggestion that he made was that the respondent's team use the project as a marketing tool for future clients as virtual reality walk-throughs have now become an integral part of the real estate business. The same, as a suggestion, was accepted. Considering the loss that the respondent's company had incurred a deferred payment term was agreed upon.

The Settlement Agreement

The Respondent agreed to pay the outstanding amount i.e. Rs. 7,88,279/- within five months, beginning December 21, 2021 till April 22, 2022, in five instalments with not a single instalment amounting to less than Rs. 1,50,000/-.

The Inference

Human consideration and creative solution providing can help resolve issues quicker.

Case Study 08

Furnishing Company Vs Handloom Distributor

Date of Claim raised:25/09/2021

Date of Conciliation: 01/10/2021

Date of Settlement: 01/10/2021

Digest: Mediation/Conciliation/Dispute/Claimant/ Respondent/Invoice/Settlement

Case Summary

This dispute occurred between a furniture manufacturer and a distributor, both based in the suburbs of Mumbai. The respondent, in this case, the distributor, was into the retail of handloom products and handicrafts and placed an order for handmade chairs and tables that he, in turn, planned to supply to a restaurant. The credit period agreed was 60 days. The delivery of products was accepted as 25 days from the date of order, and the total value of products sold was Rs. 1,58,726/-. The dispute occurred when the 60-day period had elapsed, and the commitments of payment were not honoured.

The Issue

The respondent had an incident of fire in his godown, and the same was only partially insured. In turn, he also could not supply the entire lot delivered to him by the claimant; thus, he could not fulfil his commitments. However, this was a cash loss for the claimant that needed closure. The claimant also had levied a penalty on the delay of payments with an interest of 21% p.a. The dispute was handed over to PrivateCourt for settlement.

The Process

The Mediator, once the claim was established, took up the issue with the respondent; after a few discussions, the Mediator understood that the respondent was strapped for cash flow and a single such payment would render him out of business. After a few further rounds of discussion, on humanitarian grounds, it was agreed that the penal interest would be waived off, and a deferred payment would be offered to the respondent.

The Settlement Agreement

The claimant agreed to pay the entire amount of Rs. 1,58, 726/- by paying Rs. 10,000/- on the 15th of every month starting October 2021 until the entire outstanding is cleared.

The Inference

Human considerations are often the better way to resolve issues and also ensure long business relations.

Case Study 09

Agro Giant VS Food Export Company

Date of Claim raised: 05/11/2021

Date of Conciliation: 09/11/2021

Date of Settlement: 09/11/2021

Digest: Mediation/Conciliation/Dispute/Claimant/ Respondent/Invoice/Settlement

Case Summary

This dispute is between an Agro Products manufacturing company (Claimant) and a food exporting company (Respondent), both based in Rajasthan. While the Claimant is in the business of agro-based food production, the respondent is a distributor for the same in the local and foreign markets. The deal that was struck between the two companies was that the claimant would supply the respondent with export quality material, which in turn would be white labelled by the claimant for the foreign market. A third-party company was assigned to approve quality while packing at the claimant's premises. The produce was to be supplied in three batches, and the total value of the products ordered was worth Rs. 1,00,00,000/-. While there were no advances paid and no letter of credit raised, the payments were to be made 15 days past the delivery of products at the respondent's address. While the first couple of batches arrived and were paid for, the third batch was delivered but not paid for even post 30 days from the date of delivery.

The Issue

The respondent had placed the order with the claimant based on the LC received from his overseas buyer. This LC was to be encashed Freight On Board that would take him a period of 10 days from the date of procurement of materials. The issue happened when the materials of the last batch that were stored at his facility went bad, and the produce was rejected by his buyer. The initial objection that he raised was that the product was not up to standards; hence, he denied the payment. While countered with the fact that there was a 3rd party quality approval given on his behest, the respondent ducked the discussions. The issue was addressed to PrivateCourt for settlement.

The Process

The Mediator established the legitimacy of the claim; while the discussions were initiated, the malice in the respondent's approach was evident. The mediator then explained to the respondent that the claimant could approach the Exim bodies and lodge a formal complaint and also alert the supplier's cooperatives, and this would be detrimental to the image of the respondent's company and hamper further business. Realising the difficulties that he could face, the respondent requested a deferred payment term to which the claimant agreed.

The Settlement Agreement

The Respondent agreed to pay the outstanding amount of Rs. 61,54, 041/- within 6 months from December 2021 on or before the end of June 2022.

The Inference

Understanding the intentions of parties involved in a negotiation and then manipulating a settlement at times can be tricky and made possible only by a seasoned negotiator.

Case Study 10

Furniture Manufacturer vs Furniture Trader

Date of Claim raised:08/07/2021

Date of Conciliation: 15/07/2021

Date of Settlement: 06/08/2021

Digest: Mediation/Conciliation/Dispute/Claimant/ Respondent/Invoice/Settlement

Case Summary

This dispute is between a furniture manufacturing company based out of Thane and a trader based out of Mumbai. While the manufacturer, in this case, the claimant, regularly supplied furniture to the trading company and had a long-standing relationship, there was a disagreement in the payments that needed to be made for one of the consignments. The two parties had an agreed 45-day credit period for any materials supplied, and most often, the invoices were settled within the stipulated time period. The disputed consignment was supplied on the 10th April of 2021, and a total invoice of Rs. 1,28,000/- was raised. The respondent made a payment of Rs. 1,08,000/- and refused the payment of Rs. 20,000/- and demanded that a few chairs that were supplied be accepted as a return.

The Issue/Dispute/Argument/Claim/Discourse/Disagreement/Scenario

The respondent, while asking for a return, had breached the agreed 15 day return period and had not communicated the same to the claimant within that time period. The respondent claimed that the chairs supplied were not up to the specifications that were discussed, and he will need to return the same. The claimant's stand was that the delivery was accepted by the respondent, and no complaints were made till the due date of the invoice.

The Process/Undertaking/Action

The negotiator, in this case, looked at the purchase orders and the specs given along with the same. Once the authenticity of the claim was established, a discussion with the respondent was arranged, and the negotiator tried to understand his side of the story. What came to fore was that as the goods were delivered to the respondent, the handover of the same was taken by one of his new employees who was not aware of the specs of the order. The same came to fore when the respondent, in turn sold it to his customer, which had a delay of approximately 35-days, by which time the 15-day return period had expired. Through the discussions with both sides the negotiator convinced the respondent that while the claimant understood his predicament, he would need to honour his side of the agreed terms, and in turn, the claimant agreed to supply new chars with the actual specs with an extended credit period of 60 days.

The Settlement Agreement

The Respondent agreed to pay the amount of Rs. 20,000/- in two equal of Rs. 10,000/-.

- The first instalment of Rs. 10,000/- on or before August 25. 2021.

- The second instalment of Rs. 10,000/- on or before September 29, 2021.

The Inference

Ensuring business continuity along with settling disputes is a necessary part of the goal in negotiations involving long-standing and mutually beneficial relations.

About the Author

Ankit Verma chose to debut as an author with "Dispute Resolution Via Negotiation". The book, already envisaged in his mind from the word go, he knew it was time to start manualing his thoughts and give the writer in him a chance to see the light of day.

Growing up years was fun, formative and very grounding. Ankit recalls a daily ritual that sparked his interest and concern toward law and the legal system. He recounts how every evening his father's friends would come over for a cuppa chai; they spoke, debated and discussed any and every topic that revolved around the breaking news of the day, law, politics, banking, economy, and finance. All this while he pretended to play quietly in the verandah, but his ears and mind were all drawn to their conversation. Not surprisingly, at a very young age, he had an opinion and was always trying to seek information, yearning to learn more about these topics.

Like any good son, he took up a corporate job concurrent with his education. He spent over a **decade** working the corridors of **Legal-Tech** product development and management for leading software companies across the globe, but that quiet little boy kept whispering in his ears. While still on the corporate path, he observed the overburdened legal system in the country and the lag that it created in **settling civil disputes between corporates to come to a mutual settlement**. He always thought, in most cases, a solution could have arrived without legal litigation had someone developed a platform for opposing parties to have a dialogue.

His work experience in developing tech tools for the legal framework, coupled with his experience of working with publishers of legal books in India and the U.S., aided a deeper understanding of combining the two to provide a platform that he thought was needed to set up an effective tech-based ADR system. Though this was conceptualised in 2015, he decided to immerse himself in a deeper research to ensure that the solution is nothing but perfect.

It was in 2019 when he gave up his convenient corporate life to venture into the entrepreneurial world. **His ten years plus rich legal-tech experience gave him the prowess to plan, design and execute his ambitious dream project, PrivateCourt. His main goal was to provide the best online conciliation and mediation to the corporates by launching the Dispute Resolution Paper and winning the trust and confidence of the corporates in ADR.**

Intending to provide service excellence, he hired a team of capable individuals adept at managing tech-based conciliation and mediation. The pandemic phase further catapulted the success of PrivateCourt, making the internet-averse public take steps toward online transactions and adapt themselves to this emerging reality.

Ankit, being involved in many negotiations and settlements, realised that **Conciliation** or Negotiation is an art and can't be ignored in today's business, or for that matter, even in personal life. While he has been doing his best to help businesses to settle disputes through PrivateCourt, he believes that there has to be overall enlightenment on the subject. Ankit has a strong feeling that though the matters handled for any dispute are subjective and dynamic, there is a systematic approach that can be understood as a base and can be applied in almost all matters.

This book is a humble attempt at systemising and chronically explaining the otherwise very volatile subject of Negotiation.

A visionary, marketer, product specialist, entrepreneur, and now a writer.

You can find Ankit Verma on LinkedIn - <u>Ankit Verma | LinkedIn</u>